FASTBACK® Crime and Detection

Return Payment

DAN J. MARLOWE

GLOBE FEARON
Pearson Learning Group

FASTBACK® CRIME AND DETECTION BOOKS

Beginner's Luck
The Blind Alley
Fun World
The Kid Who Sold Money
The Lottery Winner

No Loose Ends
Return Payment
The Setup
Small-Town Beat
Snowbound

Cover *t.r.* Eyewire/Getty Images, Inc. All photography © Pearson Education, Inc. (PEI) unless specifically noted.

Copyright © 2004 by Pearson Education, Inc., publishing as Globe Fearon®, an imprint of Pearson Learning Group, 299 Jefferson Road, Parsippany, NJ 07054. All rights reserved. No part of this book may be reproduced or transmitted in any form or by any means, electronic or mechanical, including photocopying, recording, or by any information storage and retrieval system, without permission in writing from the publisher. For information regarding permission(s), write to Rights and Permissions Department.

Globe Fearon® and Fastback® are registered trademarks of Globe Fearon, Inc.

ISBN 0-13-024496-1
Printed in the United States of America
1 2 3 4 5 6 7 8 9 10   07 06 05 04 03

1-800-321-3106
www.pearsonlearning.com

Arthur Bennett leaned across the desk and took the long slip of pale-green paper from Jack Blake's fingers. Then he settled back in the soft client's chair in the lawyer's office. For several seconds he just gazed respectfully at the slip of paper.

"PAY TO THE ORDER OF ARTHUR HARRINGTON BENNETT," the check read. Then came the numbers. A finely inked "5" followed by a row of five lovely zeros. "Half a million dollars," Arthur said. He liked the sound of it so much he repeated it. "Half a million dollars."

"What are you planning to do with it?" Blake asked.

"Do?" Arthur looked up from the check and saw the other man's questioning face. "Spend it," Arthur said firmly. "Enjoy it."

"Buy a few bonds? Put it in some long-term, high-interest accounts?" Blake asked.

"Perhaps. I'm not sure. I haven't really thought that much about it yet, Jack." Arthur was lying, and he was almost sure Jack Blake knew it.

A faint smile showed on the lawyer's thin lips. "In all these years, you've made no plans? After all you've been through? That's hard to believe, Arthur."

"I've always thought of it as Miriam's money, not mine," Arthur said. "I don't believe it ever really sank in that I'd wind up with it someday. I always hoped that—

well, that doesn't matter anymore, I suppose."

"I think you showed a lot of patience," Blake said.

"What choice did I have? Actually, I've wondered how *you* felt about it, Jack. We were close once. Good friends. But I thought that perhaps you blamed me, too. Like everyone else."

"Nonsense," Blake replied. "You and I are still friends, Arthur. I never thought you killed Miriam, not for one moment."

"Thanks," Arthur murmured.

"It's true, we hardly ever see each other anymore," Blake continued. "But that's my fault. Nothing to do with you. This law practice of mine keeps taking up more and more of my time. I can't play golf every weekend like we used to in the old days."

"The old days," Arthur echoed. "The old days are gone." He looked down at the check in his hand. "Not even this can bring them back. They've been gone ever since Miriam disappeared."

"I know, Arthur. But you've got to put Miriam out of your mind. You've got to start thinking about your own future."

"Yes," Arthur agreed.

That evening Arthur Bennett sat back and relaxed in his favorite leather armchair. He eased off his shoes and lit his four-dollar cigar. His first-ever four-dollar cigar. He puffed lightly and closed his eyes for a few seconds. When he opened them again, he sighed. It was a sigh of pure pleasure.

A good cigar, a favorite old chair, soft music on the stereo. Yes, it had all been worth it, he decided. The wait had been well worth it.

Seven years and two weeks—that was how long it had been since Miriam disappeared.

Miriam.

He closed his eyes and thought back to the beginning.

It had been a little sticky at first. The police nosing about, asking what seemed to be just casual questions. But behind it all, Arthur knew, they strongly suspected he was guilty of something.

"Sorry we have nothing new to report on your wife's disappearance," they would begin. Then, "By the way, Mr. Bennett, we spoke to the couple in the next apartment.

They mentioned that you and your wife had been arguing often in the last few weeks. We were wondering if you could explain...."

Arthur was pretty sure *they* were sure he'd killed her. And they certainly tried hard to build a case. But Miriam's body was never found. Finally, the police closed the case. The record stated that Miriam Bennett vanished on her own—and there was no evidence of foul play.

In spite of what the police suspected, Arthur had been very upset by Miriam's disappearance. He tried everything he could think of to find out what had happened to her. He advertised for her in the personal columns of newspapers around the state. He offered rewards for any information concerning her whereabouts. He patiently followed up dozens of tips. But they led nowhere.

He knew that he and Miriam hadn't had the perfect marriage. Far from it. But he missed her. For a long time he remained hopeful that somehow, someday she would show up again. But it never happened. So, after waiting the necessary seven years, Arthur did what anyone else in his place would have done. He went to court and had Miriam declared legally dead.

Arthur placed his half-smoked cigar in an ashtray and poured himself a glass of brandy. He swirled the amber liquid in the balloon-shaped glass and then sipped it. The taste was as good as he knew it would be. His thoughts drifted once more to his new-found wealth.

He hadn't known about Miriam's trust fund when they were first married. It wasn't until months later that he had seen the letter from her lawyer, Jack Blake, and Miriam had explained.

Her father, a wealthy manufacturer, had left his only child, Miriam, more than $400,000 in trust. Under the trust's terms, Miriam wasn't permitted to touch the money until she was 35. That meant they would have to live on the money Arthur earned. And while he made pretty good money as an insurance salesman, it wasn't enough for Miriam. The Bennetts faced ten long years of waiting for the golden goose to lay its egg.

Arthur had tried as best he could to make the marriage work. But it hadn't taken the couple long to discover that they had very little in common. Miriam was outgoing. Arthur was very shy. Miriam loved large crowds and noisy parties. Arthur preferred the peace and quiet of his living room. The surprising thing was that they had ever been attracted to each other at all.

Over the years, Miriam had become more disgusted with their lifestyle. She once even told Arthur that she'd divorce him in a minute, except for a clause in her father's will. Her father had been an old-fashioned man. He had still viewed divorce as bringing shame upon the family name. So, the will stated that if Miriam went through a divorce, she received no inheritance at all.

Miriam's constant spending finally drove them into debt. Her loud friends and louder parties battered Arthur's nerves. They found themselves fighting more and more frequently. Then, at last, the situation. . . .

The sound of the door bell interrupted Arthur's thoughts.

He set down his glass and sighed. He stubbed out his cigar and walked to the front door. He drew back the bolt and opened it. His mouth dropped and his eyes grew wide in shock. Standing in the doorway was Miriam.

She had changed, of course. Both the cut and the color of her hair were different. There were thin lines at the corners of her eyes and mouth now. But without a doubt it was Miriam. *Alive*.

"Hello, Artie," she said. "Don't you want

to give Miriam a big hug and tell her how glad you are to see her?"

Arthur stared at her, speechless. An evil smile spread across her face as she pushed past him into the apartment. "You look surprised to see me, Artie," she said. "Admit it. You *are* surprised, aren't you?"

She stood beside his chair, looking down at his ashtray and brandy glass. "Living it up, hey, Artie? I didn't think you had it in you."

Arthur was still standing by the front door. He closed it and walked into the apartment. "You're dead," he said in a daze. "All this time . . . I thought—everyone thought—you were dead. A lot of people even thought I killed you."

"I know," she said coolly. "I followed the whole thing in the papers, Artie."

"Don't call me Artie," he said. He had always hated that nickname.

"Artie! Artie!" she teased. "I was sure hoping they'd convict you. But I guess there wasn't much chance without a body. And I wasn't about to give mine up just to see you in prison. I still have a lot of living left to do. Not that I haven't had a lot of good times these past seven years."

"Why?" Arthur said in a low voice. A clinging mist seemed to be fogging his brain. *"Why?* I mean why on earth did you . . . ?" He couldn't seem to find the words he wanted.

"Why did I disappear, Artie? Or why did I come back?"

"Both," he mumbled.

"Lots of reasons," she told him. "The disappearance was because I couldn't stand living with you a single day longer. You were so *boring,* Artie. So downright boring. But mostly, I guess, the reason I disappeared was because of Jack."

Arthur found himself blinking. "Jack? You mean Jack Blake? That Jack?"

"Who else? Your old golfing pal, Artie. My lawyer. The same Jack Blake who put the check from my trust fund into your hot little hand today."

Arthur struggled to catch up. "What has—what has Jack got to do with anything, Miriam?"

She laughed, a loud shrill laugh that hurt his ears. "The whole thing was *his* idea, Artie. The *whole* thing. My disappearing and waiting this long to return. He and I became involved, and he said. . . ."

"You and Jack? You were involved with

my best friend?" Arthur shook his head. "I can't be hearing this right," he thought.

"Yes, Artie. Me and Jack. But you made it so difficult for us to spend any time together. When I managed to get away from you, you'd always call Jack to play golf or something. It got to be a real drag."

There was a sharp edge to her tone. "So Jack said the only way I could hang onto my trust fund *and* get away from you was to disappear. And I did it." She smiled wickedly. "I can tell you Jack and I have had a lot of fun, these past seven years. More fun than I would've had with you in *seventy* years."

"But . . . how . . . where have you been all this time?" Arthur finally managed to say. "How did you . . . ?"

Miriam laughed, interrupting him. "I wasn't that far away, Artie. Oh, I moved out of the state for the first several months. That was just until the newspapers stopped putting my picture on the front page. And until I was pretty sure the police had stopped looking for me. By the end of the first year, I had settled in Walken, about 150 miles from here. Jack would drive out on weekends, or else we'd meet someplace between there and here. I haven't been back to this city until tonight.

"Actually, Jack was against my coming here tonight," Miriam continued. "He said something about not rubbing your nose in it. He just wanted to handle my 'reappearance' through the courts. That's Jack—all legal and proper at all times. But I just couldn't resist coming here in person and seeing your face when you answered the door. I must say you didn't disappoint me."

Arthur was listening again, but said nothing. There was nothing he could think of to say.

"I'll bet you weren't too unhappy when I disappeared," Miriam said. "In fact, I'll bet it suited you perfectly. But then, when they started to wonder if you had killed me, that must have thrown a real scare into you."

Her voice held more than a touch of hatred in it. "Then all the fuss finally blew over, and they left you alone. I can't say I was too pleased about that, Artie. I would have been happy thinking that you were sweating it out—say for a few years."

"I didn't think you hated me that much," Arthur said.

Miriam smiled again—that same evil smile. "Tell me, Artie, how long did it take before you finally started thinking that I really *was* dead? And at the same time started dreaming about my trust fund. Dreaming about how lovely it would be if I never came back to claim it."

"You may not believe this, Miriam, but I missed you," Arthur said. "At least at first. I know we had our problems. I could never seem to make you happy. . . ."

"You can say that again," Miriam interrupted him. "But I'm sure it wasn't long before you started thinking about making *yourself* happy."

"What do you mean?" Arthur asked.

"What I mean is that you kept your fingers crossed and you waited," she went on. "And finally you convinced yourself I was dead. Jack said you would. Then three months ago my 35th birthday passed. The trust fund was mine. And last week it was exactly seven years since I disappeared. So, you hopped right into court and had me declared legally dead. And being my only surviving relative, *you* came into the trust fund. I'm sure you thought it was nice and neat the way it all worked out."

"I admit it," Arthur said. "Once I thought you were dead, I started thinking about all that money. I figured after what I went through, I was entitled to it."

"You thought that, did you, Artie?" she said angrily. "Well, that's *my* money. All of it." She paused and then smiled again.

"Actually, Jack wanted me to reappear right after my 35th birthday, when the trust fund became mine. But I talked him into waiting the extra three months. I knew you'd have me declared legally dead as soon as the seven years passed. And I wanted you to get your hands on the money—so I could take it away from you."

Suddenly all of the anger Arthur had been holding back rose to the surface. "Well, I've *got* my hands on it now," he said harshly. "And I plan on *keeping* it that way."

"Stop dreaming, Artie." Miriam said. She placed her hand on his box of cigars. "This is the last box of *anything* you'll ever buy with my money. So you'd better make them last. Jack's filing for the recovery of my trust fund tomorrow morning. Right after we have me declared legally *alive*. And as soon as the court makes you turn my money over to me, Jack's taking a leave of absence from his practice. We're taking off on a cruise around the world."

"I could kill you," Arthur said, trying hard to remain calm.

"Don't be silly," she replied briskly.

"I could kill you right now," he insisted. "It wouldn't be murder. You're already legally dead. I could kill you and get rid of your body."

Miriam was shaking her head. "Would

you believe Jack even thought of that possibility? But we talked it over and decided you weren't the type. You couldn't do it."

They knew him too well, Arthur realized. He couldn't even put a scare into her. They knew him better than he knew himself. Between the two of them. . . .

The door bell sounded again.

"Expecting company, Artie?" Miriam asked. "You didn't invite a woman here tonight to help you celebrate, did you?" she teased.

Arthur ignored her and went over to open the door. Standing there was Jack Blake. He gave Arthur a quick glance, then looked past him and straight at Miriam.

"I was afraid I'd find you here," he said to her. "Couldn't you just leave it alone and do it in court as I wanted?"

"Relax, Jack," Miriam said a little annoyed. "Artie and I were just having a friendly chat. And I think he's taking this sudden turn of events rather well. At least he hasn't fainted yet," she laughed.

"Did you really hate me that much, Jack?" Arthur asked. "Leading me on for *seven years*. And then waiting until I even got my hands on the money...."

"No," Blake said quickly. "I didn't want to drag it out more than was necessary. I...."

"I told you the extra touches were *my* idea," Miriam interrupted.

"With me it was strictly business," Blake continued. "I wanted Miriam to get what was coming to her. You can understand that, can't you?"

"Sure," Arthur thought, "strictly business." Arthur had been married to Miriam, and Jack Blake wanted her. So he thought of a plan to have her *and* her money. Maybe the money part made it a business deal for Jack.

"All right, you two have had your fun," Arthur said angrily. "Now why don't you get out of here."

"Now don't be bitter, Artie," Miriam said. "We'll be on our way. But why don't you make it easier for us, and just endorse that check over to me. It would save us some extra time in court."

Arthur felt as if he would explode. "Miriam, your nerve continues to amaze me. You want that money, you go to court and try to get it." He pointed at Jack and said, "You've got yourself a lawyer here. Well, I'll get one, too. Then we'll see how easy it will be to get my money."

"It's *my* money," Miriam said. "As long as I can prove who I am, I'll get it back. Right, Jack?"

"She's right, Arthur," Blake said. "Don't waste your money getting a lawyer and fighting us. You'll only be making a big mistake."

"The only mistakes I've made in my life were marrying Miriam and picking you for a best friend. Now get out of my apartment."

"Come on, Jack," Miriam said. "Let's leave him alone with his fancy cigars and expensive brandy. We'll give him one night to enjoy his good fortune. See you in court, Artie," she said, taking Blake's hand.

As they walked toward the door, Jack turned and said, "I'm sorry, Arthur. Better luck next time." They went out and closed the door behind them.

Arthur went over and bolted the lock. Then he walked slowly across the living room to his bedroom. He went inside and sat down on the bed. He knew there was only one thing he could do now. Miriam and Jack hadn't left him any choice.

He got up and pulled the two suitcases out from under his bed. He unlocked them and stood staring down at the neatly stacked piles of bills. Two suitcases filled to the top with one-hundred-dollar bills. A total of $500,000.

For the first time all evening, Arthur smiled.

He thought of what he had said to Jack. "The only mistakes I've made in my life were marrying Miriam and picking you for a best friend." Well, that wasn't really true. He had made plenty of other mistakes in his life. But *today*—today made up for all of them.

At the time, he hadn't even known *why* he wanted to cash the check that very afternoon. The bank had certainly been against it. "You'd be making a big mistake carrying all that cash around, Mr. Bennett," they'd said.

But Arthur had insisted—all the way up to the bank's vice-president. "I just want the cash for tonight," he'd told the woman. "I'll bring it back tomorrow for you to put into some safe accounts. But tonight I want the cash. I've been waiting for it for a long time."

They had finally given in. First they called the issuing bank to make sure the check was OK. Then they had to send out to two other branches to get all the hundred-dollar bills Arthur wanted. Two bank guards helped Arthur load his suitcases and even walked him to his car.

Well, Arthur *had* intended to return tomorrow and open some accounts at that bank. But tonight's events had forced a change of plans.

He went into his closet and pulled down another suitcase from the shelf. He began to pack it with clothes as quickly as he could. As he did, he thought of Miriam and Jack.

He had been very tempted to show them the money before they left. Just to see the shocked look on their faces. He could guess Miriam's reaction—pure anger. As for Jack, he would have trouble believing that Arthur would have been bold enough to get the $500,000 in cash in one day. Not meek, mild Arthur.

Well, he'd passed up the chance to see them squirm a little. But that was OK. He wasn't taking any risks. With Miriam pushing Jack, they might have done something desperate. Like knocking Arthur out and stealing the money. This way was safer—and cleaner.

Tomorrow, all the legal forces Jack Blake could reach would begin looking for Arthur Bennett. Except Arthur Bennett wouldn't be there.

In an hour he would be at the airport. In another four hours he would be out of anyone's reach. South America suddenly sounded very good.

Miriam and Jack liked to play disappearing games, did they?

Very well, a disappearing game is what he would give them.

DAN J. MARLOWE *is the author of more than 25 adventure and suspense novels. He's a past winner of the Mystery Writers of America's prestigious Edgar Allan Poe Award.*